T0376410

AMAZING SCIENCE
EARTH WONDERS

Written by Alex Hall

Genius Kid

American adaptation copyright © 2026 by North Star Editions, Mendota Heights, MN 55120. All rights reserved. No part of this book may be reproduced or utilized in any form or by any means without written permission from the publisher.

Earth Wonders © 2024 BookLife Publishing
This edition is published by arrangement with BookLife Publishing

sales@northstareditions.com | 888-417-0195

Library of Congress Control Number:
2024952959

ISBN
978-1-952455-25-4 (library bound)
978-1-952455-81-0 (paperback)
978-1-952455-63-6 (epub)
978-1-952455-45-2 (hosted ebook)

Printed in the United States of America
Mankato, MN
092025

Written by:
Alex Hall

Edited by:
Elise Carraway

Designed by:
Ker Ker Lee

All facts, statistics, web addresses and URLs in this book were verified as valid and accurate at time of writing. No responsibility for any changes to external websites or references can be accepted by either the author or publisher.

Photo Credits – Images courtesy of Shutterstock.com, unless otherwise stated.

Cover – Rubi Rodriguez Martinez, Marti Bug Catcher, ladavie, tawin bunkoed, ON-Photography Germany, Anna Nikonorova, Daniel Prudek, Theresa J Graham, Umit Yildiz. 2–3 – vitormarigo, Marti Bug Catcher. 4–5 – Photoongraphy, Marti Bug Catcher, New Africa. 6–7 – Wirestock Creators, Alex Staroseltsev, HilaryDesign, Peter Hermes Furian. 8–9 – Inna photographer, Marti Bug Catcher, romeovip_md. 10–11 – Alberto Masnovo, Vixit. 12–13 – Marti Bug Catcher, Daniel Levin Bennett, Nicolas Primola, Alberto Masnovo, Bossa Art. 14–15 – Allexxandar, Sergieiev, Cynthia A Jackson, Izen Kai. 16–17 – Marti Bug Catcher, Sergii Figurnyi, Richard Hages. 18–19 – Mumemories, Rolau Elena, Nganhaycuoi. 20–21 – Sopotnicki, glebantiy, a_v_d, Nemanja Petronje. 22–23 – Ground Picture, Marti Bug Catcher, STUDIO DREAM.

CONTENTS

Page 4   Earth Wonders
Page 6   Key Words
Page 8   Canyons
Page 10   Mountains
Page 12   Volcanoes
Page 14   Coral Reefs
Page 16   Waterfalls
Page 18   Northern Lights
Page 20   Believe It or Not!
Page 22   Are You a Genius Kid?
Page 24   Glossary and Index

Words that look like this can be found in the glossary on page 24.

EARTH WONDERS

Have you ever wondered why we have waterfalls? Maybe you have pondered over what makes a mountain.

Natural wonders are places and events in the world that amaze people. These wonders are not made by humans.

Earth is full of many natural wonders. People from around the world visit natural wonders every year.

DID YOU KNOW?
Most natural wonders have been around for millions of years.

Have you ever been wowed by something in the natural world?

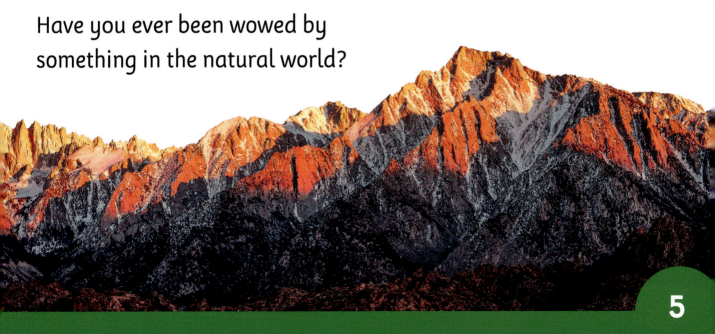

KEY WORDS

Here are some key words about Earth wonders that every genius kid should learn.

EROSION
Erosion is when water or wind wears rock or soil away.

POLES
The poles are the most northern and southern points on Earth.

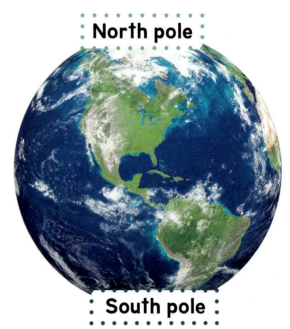

North pole

South pole

CONTINENTS

Continents are large areas of land. There are seven continents. Continents are split into smaller areas called countries.

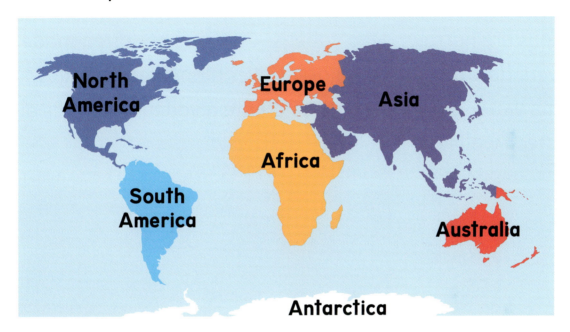

TECTONIC PLATES

Tectonic plates are large moving pieces of rock underground that make up Earth.

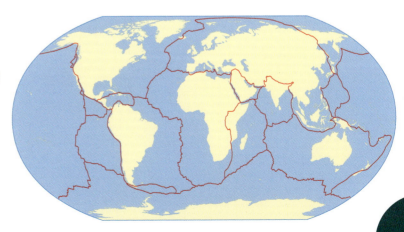

CANYONS

Canyons are narrow, deep <u>valleys</u>. Canyons are often made by rivers flowing over rocky areas over many years. The flowing water erodes the rock to create a valley. It carves out tall, steep walls.

Canyon walls have different layers of rock. The different layers can show us what Earth was like millions of years ago.

The Grand Canyon in North America is one of the longest canyons on Earth. It is almost 280 miles long!

MOUNTAINS

A mountain is a patch of land that rises above the ground surrounding it.

Mountains are made when tectonic plates move. The plates push together. Then the land crumples upwards.

DID YOU KNOW?
The top of a mountain is called the peak or summit.

Land has to be at least 984 feet high to be a mountain.

A group of mountains close together is called a mountain range. The world's highest mountain range is the Himalayas in Asia.

Mount Everest is in the Himalayas. It is the highest mountain on Earth. It is 29,032 feet high.

VOLCANOES

Volcanoes are openings in Earth's surface.

Deep inside Earth, there is a very hot liquid called magma. Magma is melted rock. When magma escapes from a volcano, it is called an eruption.

DID YOU KNOW?
Magma becomes lava when it reaches Earth's surface.

There are three types of volcanoes.

ACTIVE VOLCANOES
Active volcanoes regularly erupt. They are likely to erupt again.

Mount Etna

Mount Kilimanjaro

DORMANT VOLCANOES
Dormant volcanoes have not erupted for a long time. But they may erupt again.

Ben Nevis

EXTINCT VOLCANOES
Extinct volcanoes will not erupt again.

CORAL REEFS

Coral reefs are colorful. They are made up of many living creatures called coral polyps.

Coral reefs are home to many other living things. More living things live in coral reefs than in any other part of the ocean.

Coral reefs are found in <u>shallow</u>, warm waters all over the world.

The Great Barrier Reef is near Australia. It is the largest coral reef in the world.

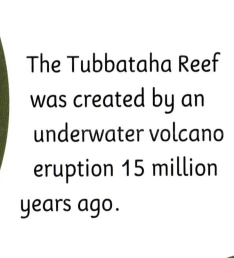

The Tubbataha Reef was created by an underwater volcano eruption 15 million years ago.

WATERFALLS

Waterfalls are places where water drops down.

Most waterfalls are created by rivers. The rivers flow over rocks. Some rocks are harder than other rocks. The rivers wear down the soft rocks. Then only hard rocks are left. The water continues to flow over the edges to create waterfalls.

Niagara Falls is a group of three huge waterfalls between Canada and the United States.

Victoria Falls Rainforest

Victoria Falls in Africa is the largest waterfall in the world. Victoria Falls is next to a rainforest. The water spray from the falls makes it rain in the rainforest all day, every day.

NORTHERN LIGHTS

The northern lights create a colorful light show in the sky. The lights are caused by storms and winds from the sun.

These storms send out lots of tiny <u>particles</u>. These particles get pulled toward Earth by the <u>magnetic</u> pull from the north and south poles.

When these particles mix with air, they make bright colors. They are often green, red, blue, or purple.

The northern lights are also known as the aurora borealis. They can mainly be seen near the north pole at certain times of year.

BELIEVE IT OR NOT!

Volcanoes can be helpful! Lava and ash can create soil that is full of <u>nutrients</u>. This soil helps plants grow.

Earth's first coral reefs formed hundreds of millions of years ago. They were around before dinosaurs!

In 1901, Annie Edson Taylor went over Niagara Falls in a barrel. The most surprising thing is that she survived!

Rainbows are a common but amazing Earth wonder. Rainbows happen when sunlight passes through raindrops.

ARE YOU A GENIUS KID?

Now you are full of amazing Earth wonder facts. Who will you impress with all your knowledge? Before you go, let's test what you have learned. Are you really a genius kid?

Check back through the book if you are not sure.

1. How are canyons usually created?
2. What is the name for the type of volcano that is most likely to erupt again?
3. What is the largest waterfall in the world?

Answers:
1. By rivers eroding the rocks, 2. An active volcano, 3. Victoria Falls.

GLOSSARY

magnetic — to be able to pull or stick to certain items with an invisible force

nutrients — natural substances that plants and animals need to grow and stay healthy

particles — tiny things that are too small to see

shallow — not very deep

valleys — low areas of land between hills or mountains, often with rivers flowing through them

INDEX

continents 7
erosion 6, 8
lava 12, 20
magma 12
mountains 4, 10–11
oceans 14
particles 18–19
rainbows 21
rock 6–9, 12, 16
tectonic plates 7, 10